Teaching with iPad How-To

Use your iPad creatively for everyday teaching tasks in schools and universities

Shubhangi Harsha

Sumit Kataria

BIRMINGHAM - MUMBAI

Teaching with iPad How-To

First published: November 2012

Production Reference: 1011112

Published by Packt Publishing Ltd.
Livery Place
35 Livery Street
Birmingham B3 2PB, UK.

ISBN 978-1-84969-442-1

www.packtpub.com

Credits

Authors

Shubhangi Harsha

Sumit Kataria

Reviewer

Silvina P. Hillar

Acquisition Editor

Joanna Finchen

Commissioning Editor

Maria D'souza

Technical Editor

Prasanna Joglekar

Project Coordinator

Esha Thakker

Proofreader

Aaron Nash

Production Coordinator

Prachali Bhiwandkar

Cover Work

Prachali Bhiwandkar

Cover Image

Aditi Gajjar

About the Authors

Shubhangi Harsha professionally develops iPad, iPhone, and Android applications. She understands the heart and soul of the mobile application development and likes to create challenging apps that are data-heavy and dynamic in nature.

Shubhangi studied Computer Science and Engineering in her bachelors studies at PEC University of Technology, Chandigarh, India and graduated from there in 2010 as the topper of all branches in the University. She is a student of M.Sc. in Computing at Imperial College London, for which she has been awarded the prestigious Jubilee Scholarship of the British Council and the Government of the United Kingdom.

Shubhangi likes to take up mind games in her free time. She likes to anchor cultural events and is passionate about dancing. A non-trained dancer, she has given numerous solo stage performances in dance and mimicry too. She is very close to her parents and loves to spend time with them. Awarded the title of "All-Rounder Girl" during her studies, Shubhangi likes to explore her capabilities in diverse areas, and authoring this book is another such exploration. This is her first book, written with the motive of helping school teachers who choose to use the iPad.

On fast-pace successful completion of my first book, I pay my sincere thanks and gratitude to my parents, Dr. H.K. Verma and Mrs. Usha Verma, who brought me up and educated me in a way that today I find myself capable enough to author a book that can make imparting of knowledge both interesting and convenient. Thank you mom and dad for co-operating with me in all possible ways and for not disturbing my sleep till noon everyday when I worked in the night to write this book and manage my other work alongside.

I feel fortunate to have some close, true, and special friends who selflessly encouraged and supported me in everything I chose to do, even to write this book. My special thanks to my co-author, Sumit Kataria, for being a great co-worker.

I appreciate the entire Packt team for their professional yet friendly handling of the writing and publishing of this book. Lastly, I thank all the fantastic people who have chosen to read my first book and shall be grateful to receive their valuable comments and feedback.

Sumit Kataria is a software engineer and technology enthusiast who trusts in open source software. He possesses both a deep knowledge of Drupal programming and magical mobile app development skills allowing him to make Drupal and mobile sing together in beautiful harmony.

Sumit has built more than 20 iPhone/iPad/Android social-networking / ecommerce / media apps. He has worked with Lullabot, CommerceGuys, and CivicActions building several large-scale CMS integrated mobile applications, including the Kickstart mobile commerce, Drupalize.Me, and Do It With Drupal conference app.

Sumit is very passionate about everything he does and tries to bring the same enthusiasm to his projects. He has been a presenter at 4 DrupalCons and several DrupalCamps, advocating Drupal as a mobile application cloud-based backend. He was a Google Summer of Code student for Drupal in 2008, and has been managing the whole program ever since.

When Sumit is not working on Drupal/Mobile, he enjoys traveling and exploring new places. Sumit lives in New Delhi, India. Find him on LinkedIn (`http://bit.ly/sumitk01`), on Twitter as `@sumitk`, or mail at `sumitk@sumitk.net`.

This book is dedicated to my mom and dad, Indu and Subhash for their continuous support, my uncle Arun, sisters Nidhi and Shivani for always believing in me, and to all my close friends Anuj, Ankush, Dhruv, Manisha, Shubhangi, and many more. Shubhangi is also co-author of this book, whose amazing dedication and effort kept us on schedule.

Team at Packt - Amber, Esha, Manali, and Maria for making this project such a smooth ride. And finally to you, awesome reader, for buying this book.

About the Reviewer

Silvina P. Hillar is an Italian who has been teaching English since 1993. She has always had a great interest in teaching, writing, and composing techniques, and has made a lot of research on this subject. She has been investigating and using mind mapping for more than 10 years in order to embed it into teaching.

She is an English Teacher, a Certified Legal Translator (English/Spanish), and has a Post Graduate Degree in Education (graduated with Honors).

She has been working in several schools and institutes with native English speaking students and as an independent consultant for many international companies as an interpreter, translator, and VLE (Virtual Learning Environment) course designer.

She has always had a passion for technological devices concerning education. Former videos and cassettes were a must in her teaching lessons, and computers were and still are present. Her brother Gastón C. Hillar designed some programs and games for her teaching. Lately, she is teaching using Moodle and Web 2.0. Previously for Packt, Silvina has written *Moodle 1.9 English Teacher's Cookbook*, *Moodle 2.0 Multimedia Cookbook*, and *Mindmapping with FreeMind*. She believes that one of the most amazing challenges in education is bridging the gap between classic education and modern technologies.

She has been doing a lot of research on multimedia assets which enhance the teaching and learning through VLE platforms. She tries to embed the learning of students through new resources which are appealing and innovative for them. Thus, multimedia stimulates the different thinking skills as well as multiple intelligencies.

www.PacktPub.com

Support files, eBooks, discount offers and more

You might want to visit www.PacktPub.com for support files and downloads related to your book.

Did you know that Packt offers eBook versions of every book published, with PDF and ePub files available? You can upgrade to the eBook version at www.PacktPub.com and as a print book customer, you are entitled to a discount on the eBook copy. Get in touch with us at service@packtpub.com for more details.

At www.PacktPub.com, you can also read a collection of free technical articles, sign up for a range of free newsletters and receive exclusive discounts and offers on Packt books and eBooks.

http://PacktLib.PacktPub.com

Do you need instant solutions to your IT questions? PacktLib is Packt's online digital book library. Here, you can access, read and search across Packt's entire library of books.

Why Subscribe?

- ▶ Fully searchable across every book published by Packt
- ▶ Copy and paste, print and bookmark content
- ▶ On demand and accessible via web browser

Free Access for Packt account holders

If you have an account with Packt at www.PacktPub.com, you can use this to access PacktLib today and view nine entirely free books. Simply use your login credentials for immediate access.

Table of Contents

Preface 1

Teaching with iPad How-To 5

Planning your lessons (Must know) 5

Keeping your notes (Must know) 9

Creating presentations and charts (Must know) 13

Carrying your textbooks (Must know) 18

Recording attendance and student profiles (Must know) 21

Making quick references (Must know) 25

Using projectors and interacting (Must know) 28

Connecting with your subject (Must know) 31

Creating and managing timetables (Must know) 39

Interactive books for kids (Should know) 42

Educating students with special needs (Should know) 46

Teaching art, craft, and practical skills (Should know) 50

Teaching music on iPad (Advanced) 54

Teaching using 3D resources (Advanced) 57

Publishing your learning material (Advanced) 61

Learning iPad tips and tricks (Advanced) 65

iTunes U (Advanced) 68

Preface

Teaching, as we like to say, is an art. This book is aimed at introducing the iPad as a teaching tool for teachers to create a wonderful piece of art, called the class, every day with their students. The iPad can make routine tasks such as attendance recording and notes management, much easier. It can make classes interesting, engrossing, and highly interactive for students. The book is organized into various recipes and each recipe focuses on one such different task that can be performed conveniently on your iPad.

What this book covers

Planning your lessons (Must know), will take you through the Planbook application, using which you can carry out your regular lesson planning on your iPad.

Keeping your notes (Must know), is aimed at making your management of notes easier by syncing them and accessing them everywhere using the Evernote app. You can also put pictures, links, and other resources associated to your topic with your notes.

Creating presentations and charts (Must know), will explain how the Keynote app on your iPad can be used to create and share interactive presentations and 3D charts.

Carrying your textbooks (Must know), will talk about accessing your textbooks and other reference books through the iBooks application. It will discuss the additional features such as quick references and interactive images that you get with these eBooks.

Recording attendance and student profiles (Must know), will enable you to make the cumbersome task of attendance and student behavior recording easier by using the Teacher's Assistant Pro app.

Making quick references (Must know), is aimed at making you comfortable with Safari and its various features, so you can have a quick, handy lookup during your class or outside whenever you need to. It will also talk about accessing the dictionary and encyclopedia on your iPad.

Using Projectors and Interacting (Must know), lists all the requirements for projecting the content of your iPad on a display monitor for the entire class and explains how to do it.

Connecting with your subject (Must know), will cover popular, subject specific applications available in the App Store. This chapter will, in detail, talk about apps of basic subjects such as mathematics and science, and how they can help in making your class more interesting.

Creating and managing timetables (Must know), will talk about creating weekly timetables and schedules, and distributing them to students via e-mail. It will explain the Classes Lite application that is suitable for you, even if you are teaching multiple classes.

Interactive books for kids (Should know), will explain how you can create interactive eBooks for kids using the Demibooks® Composer app. The chapter will also introduce some interactive eBooks for kids, which are available in the App Store.

Educating students with special needs (Should know), will talk about how an iPad can be used to improve the communication skills and other learning aspects of children suffering from dyslexia and autism.

Teaching art, craft, and practical skills (Should know), will describe apps such as Animation Desk™, Procreate – Sketch, paint, create, SketchBook Pro, and how you can create and teach to create wonderful pieces of art through these apps.

Teaching music on iPad (Advanced), will tell you how the little device can be converted into a number of musical instruments such as a piano, guitar, drums, and so on. It also talks about recording your and your students' musical creations and referring to them later when required.

Teaching using 3D resources (Advanced), is aimed at making classes interesting and interactive for your students. It discusses few applications that use 3D modeling very aptly to teach some of the toughest subjects.

Publishing your learning material (Advanced), is aimed at giving you the power to create your own multimedia eBooks, make them interactive, and publish them for your students.

Learning iPad tips and tricks (Advanced), will take you through an app called Tips and Tricks - iPad Secrets. This app will tell you about some known and lesser-known features of the iPad that can make your regular work quick and easy.

iTunes U (Advanced), will talk about accessing organized coursework from around the world over your iPad. It will also talk about how you can publish and distribute your own coursework.

What you need for this book

As we are going to talk about teaching with the amazing device called the iPad, all you need is to have access to one. The only other thing you are expected to do of, is to have the basic know-how of searching and downloading an application from the App Store onto your iPad.

Who this book is for

If you are a teacher or going to become one, and want your classes to be interesting and informative, then this book will definitely be of use to you. The book talks about how you can bring some organization and ease into your teaching profession with the help of an iPad. It is for teachers teaching at all levels of the education system, from nursery to university, who are willing to benefit from the convenience that modern-day technology has to offer.

Conventions

In this book, you will find a number of styles of text that distinguish between different kinds of information. Words that you see on the screen, in menus or dialog boxes for example, appear in the text like this: "To start creating lesson plans you need to choose the option **Create New Planbook** or import one from your dropbox folder."

Reader feedback

Feedback from our readers is always welcome. Let us know what you think about this book—what you liked or may have disliked. Reader feedback is important for us to develop titles that you really get the most out of.

To send us general feedback, simply sendan e-mail to `feedback@packtpub.com`, and mention the book title viathe subject of your message.

If there is a book that you need and would like to see us publish, please send us a note in the **SUGGEST A TITLE** form on `www.packtpub.com` or e-mail `suggest@packtpub.com`.

If there is a topic that you have expertise in and you are interested in either writing or contributing to a book, see our author guide on `www.packtpub.com/authors`.

Customer support

Now that you are the proud owner of a Packt book, we have a number of things to help you to get the most from your purchase.

Errata

Although we have taken every care to ensure the accuracy of our content, mistakes do happen. If you find a mistake in one of our books—maybe a mistake in the text or the code—we would be grateful if you would report this to us. By doing so, you can save other readers from frustration and help us improve subsequent versions of this book. If you find any errata, please report them by visiting `http://www.packtpub.com/support`, selecting your book, clicking on the **erratasubmissionform** link, and entering the details of your errata. Once your errata are verified, your submission will be accepted and the errata will be uploaded on our website, or added to any list of existing errata, under the Errata section of that title. Any existing errata can be viewed by selecting your title from `http://www.packtpub.com/support`.

Piracy

Piracy of copyright material on the Internet is an ongoing problem across all media. At Packt, we take the protection of our copyright and licenses very seriously. If you come across any illegal copies of our works, in any form, on the Internet, please provide us with the location address or website name immediately so that we can pursue a remedy.

Please contact us at `copyright@packtpub.com` with a link to the suspected pirated material.

We appreciate your help in protecting our authors, and our ability to bring you valuable content.

Questions

You can contact us at `questions@packtpub.com` if you are having a problem with any aspect of the book, and we will do our best to address it.

Teaching with iPad How-To

iPad is a device that fascinates not only gadget-loving people but also teachers and professionals alike, for its varied applications coupled with great screen and looks. This book is organized into various recipes and in each recipe we will focus on a task that you as a teacher have to do regularly. We will also look at the apps that can make imparting knowledge convenient and more interesting for all teachers and their students.

Planning your lessons (Must know)

Planning lessons is one of the main tasks a teacher has to perform almost every single day. There are many apps available for this purpose for the iPad. Let us choose the Planbook app here because it makes it very easy to create, modify, and share plans. Its user interface is pretty illustrative and it is definitely a good app to start with even if you are not comfortable and proficient with iPad apps.

Getting ready

We begin by downloading the Planbook app from the App Store. It costs $9.99 but is definitely worth the money spent. You may also like to download its Mac app from Mac App Store, if you wish to keep your iPad and Mac in sync.

How to do it...

1. The home screen of the app shows the available Planbooks, but as it is your first launch of the app there will be no available Planbooks. To start creating lesson plans you need to choose the option **Create New Planbook** or import one from your dropbox folder.

2. Planbook provides excellent customization features to suit your exact needs. You can add as many courses as you want by clicking on **Add Courses**. You can specify the dates in the **Dates you want included in your Planbook** textbox as a date range, and even select the type of schedule you use as illustrated in the next screenshot:

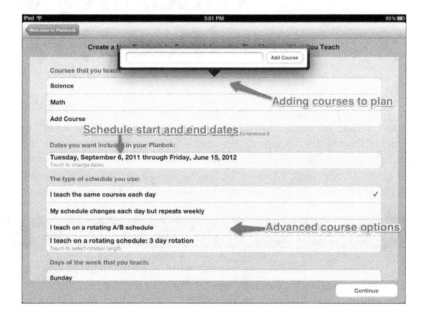

3. Now that you have specified the major features of your plan, you need to click on **Continue** to specify the time range of each course of a day. Planbook provides standard iOS date pickers to choose start and end times for each course. After putting in all details for a lesson plan, you need to click on **Continue**, which will take you back to the home screen, where you can now see the Planbook you just made in the list of available files. If you wish to, you can edit the name of your Planbook, delete it, or e-mail it. As we want to move forward to create your detailed plan, you should select **Open Planbook File** of your plan.

4. You should now see your lesson plan for one entire week. Each course is represented by a different color for each day, and its contents are shown at the very same place minimizing unnecessary navigation.

5. As you have created the complete outline of your lesson plan, it is time you should specify the content of each course. It's easy—just tap on the course you want to create content for, and a screen with many user-friendly customization features will appear. This is shown in the next screenshot:

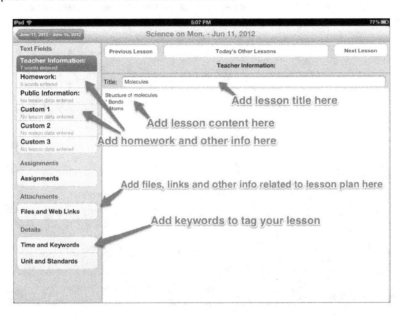

Here you can enter your course content divided into six different text fields in the **Text Fields** column at the right-hand side, with even the title of each field being editable! You can specify assignments in the textbox **Assignments** for the course, use attachments in **Files and Web Links** in the **Attachments** option related to the course content, and even have keywords in **Keywords** which might help you with easy look up.

6. If you wish to see your lesson plan on the basis of a single day, simply click on **Day** tab at the bottom as shown in the following screenshot and you will see a nice, clean day plan. Tapping on the course still works to edit it! You can tap on a course with two fingers if you want to view it in detail. You will find this small feature very useful when you need to have a quick look at the course content while in class.

7. One of the reasons I was so impressed with this app was the set of powerful editing and navigation options it provides. The gear icon at the bottom-right corner of each course pops up a box of tools. You can use this box to:

   ❑ **Bump Lesson**: You can shift the course further by one day using this option. The course content for the selected day becomes blank.

   ❑ **Yank Lesson**: This option removes the course for the selected day. The entire course shifts back by one day.

□ **Make Non-School Day**: This option gets either all the courses of the day shifted further by one day or the content of all courses of the day is deleted, depending on the user's choice.

8. You have a **Courses** button in the top-right corner, which lets you show/hide courses in the plan. You also have a **Share** button besides the **Courses** button that will let you print or e-mail the Planbook, in a day-wise or week-wise arrangement depending on the active tab.

9. To navigate between weeks/days, swipe from the left- to right-hand side or from the right- to left-hand side to move to the previous or next week/day respectively. You can also click on the **Week** or **Day** options present at the bottom of the screen to navigate to that particular week/day.

How it works...

We have now created a Planbook as per your requirements. You can create multiple Planbooks in the same way. The Planbook app saves each Planbook as a file on the device that you can retrieve, modify, and delete at any later stage even when you are offline.

There's more...

The iPad App Store has many other apps apart from Planbook (which we chose due to its simplicity and powerful features) that facilitate planning lessons. There is an app My LessonPlan, which costs $2.99, but is more advantageous in classes where even students have access to personal devices. iPlanLessons, costing $6.99 is another powerful app and can be considered as an alternative to Planbook.

Keeping your notes (Must know)

Wouldn't it be great to capture notes, save research, collaborate on projects, snap photos of whiteboards, record audio, and do much more with just one tool? The Evernote app, which is one of the most popular pieces of software provides all such facilities. It is available for iOS, Android, Mac, and PC and anything added to your account is automatically synced and made available on all your devices.

Getting ready

We begin by downloading the free Evernote app from the App Store. You might also like to download its Mac/PC apps as well if you wish to keep your iPad and Mac/PC in sync. After download log in with your existing Evernote account or create a new one.

How to do it...

1. You can start by creating new notebook for each subject you teach and then start adding notes under them. Just tap on the **New note** button in the bottom-left corner of your screen to start creating a new note. You can now give an appropriate title to your note and select the notebook you wish to add it to. You can also add tags (to organize content well), textual content, pictures, or recorded media to your note. Click on **Save** in the top-right corner to save it. The note you just created will appear under selected notebook and will sync across all your devices.

2. To review all notes under a particular notebook, tap on the **Notebooks** tab present at the top of the home screen and select a particular subject's notebook. You can now see all your subject notes. A sleek search bar in the top-right corner of the screen enables you to look for content within notes and images whenever you wish to. This is shown in the next screenshot:

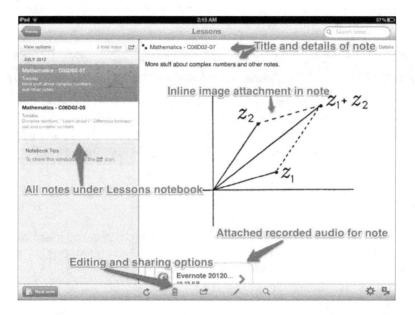

Now that you know how to create and find notes, we should look closely at adding content to notes and editing it. One of the most exciting features of Evernote is that it can access different kinds of media.

3. To open a note and add content to it, just tap on it and use the editing options at the bottom of the screen.

In Evernote you can do something more than usual with text also. You can use advanced editing options of the inbuilt editor (which opens by default) to customize text. These options include font settings such as bold, italic, underline, and text options such as hyperlink, and so on.

4. Taking pictures of whiteboard and adding them to lesson notes is a great way of organizing notes. To add pictures to your note, use the **Camera** and **Images** buttons, shown as icons present on the top bar of the note view. **Camera** lets you take pictures on the spot and add them while the **Images** button opens the device gallery of saved pictures. Look at the following screenshot:

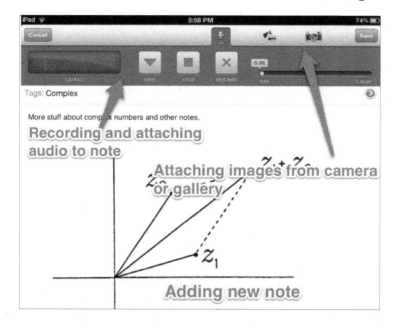

It is very easy to record lectures with the **Mike** button on the top bar. The recorded piece of audio is automatically attached to the selected note.

5. Once you are done editing your note, click on the **Save** button on the top-right corner. Evernote exhibits its most powerful feature here and syncs your note across all available devices attached to your account!

   Evernote also lets you share your note on Facebook, Twitter, or via e-mail right from within the app. It also gives you the option to print a note via air print. These options can be exercised with the **Share** button present at the center of the bottom bar and are helpful for distributing notes to students and collaborating with teachers to develop better course content.

6. To see more details about a created note, tap on **Details** within notes view. It provides you information about notebook, tags, created date, last updated date, geo data, and more.

Evernote desktop apps for Mac and PC also let you import PDF files and attach .doc files within notes. The next screenshot shows this syncing:

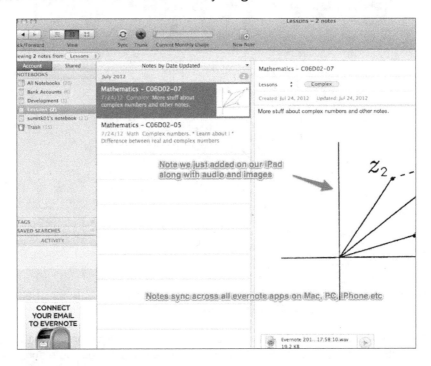

How it works...

Adding content to a note links all text and media to that particular note file and links the note file to a notebook. This content is kept in a user's Evernote account and some data is stored locally on the device too. When a user logs in to his/her Evernote account on any device, all notes are synced and brought to that device, irrespective of where the note was created.

There's more...

For most of the users using Evernote free account is fine. But if you would like to allow collaborators to edit and modify notebooks that are shared with them, you will require a premium subscription. For schools and teachers there is discount under educational rate.

Creating notes via e-mail

You can also create notes by sending an e-mail to Evernote. If you tag your e-mail in the prescribed format these notes will get added to designated notebooks. You can get your Evernote e-mail under **Settings | Evernote email address**. If you don't tag your e-mail it will end up in your default notebook.

Making handwritten notes searchable

Image recognition makes handwritten notes searchable on Evernote. This is ideal for teachers as they make lots of notes by hand.

Creating presentations and charts (Must know)

Making presentations is one of the most successful teaching methods in the industry and is being speedily adopted by many new teachers around the globe. The Keynote app is the most powerful tool to create presentations on iPad. It utilizes the multi touch technology of iPad very well to create great looking presentations with pictures, charts, and animations.

Getting ready

Let's begin by shelling out $9.99 and downloading the very useful Keynote app from the App Store.

How to do it...

1. As soon as you launch the app, you will find 12 themes to give you a great start. Each theme comes with coordinated fonts, colors, backgrounds, and images. Tap on the theme you wish to choose and you will be taken to the view of creating main presentation. You should now be able to see the first slide of your presentation which will also be the cover slide.

2. To add a new slide to your presentation, tap on the Add (**+**) button at the bottom of list of slides and choose a slide template from the available options. These templates are pre-made content arrangement patterns. You can choose the blank template if you wish to make your own content arrangement. Look at the next screenshot:

3. The left-hand side column on your screen is the navigator. You can use this space to change order of slides or copy and delete them. Navigator displays a thumbnail image of each slide. To move a slide, select it and drag-and-drop it at the destination position. You can even select multiple slides using multi-touch and move them together.

4. Before you begin to add content to your presentation slides, it will be good to have a look at the four basic editing options present at the top-right space of your screen. These buttons are shown in the next screenshot:

5. Let us now start playing with the content of our presentation. Adding text and modifying it is pretty simple—just double-tap on the text area and it becomes editable!

   To deselect the object, tap anywhere and to now paste this object, tap on the background and then tap on Paste. This object becomes movable and you can place it wherever you like.

   To resize an object, tap on it and you will see selection handles appear. Drag these handles to achieve desired size. To match an object size with another one on the same slide, select it and tap on other object. You can also zoom on a particular section of an image using pinch by two fingers. To rotate your slide objects twist with two fingers.

6. Let's start formatting objects in our slides. To format an object, tap on the object and then tap on the **Format** button. You can choose from the list of available styles to give your object the desired look.

7. As a teacher, creating charts might be an important task for you. In Keynote, you can create charts, not only of different types, but also 3D charts. To create a chart, use the **Insert** button. Look at the next screenshot:

To edit the data of a chart tap on the chart, when it gets selected, tap on **Edit Data** and a data editor will be revealed where you can enter your chart values.

To take advantage of 3D charts you should know how to rotate them. Tap on the chart. It will get selected and now you can drag your finger over the Rotate Zone that shows up (it can be seen at the center of the diagram that follows). Your chart can now be rotated in the 3D space!

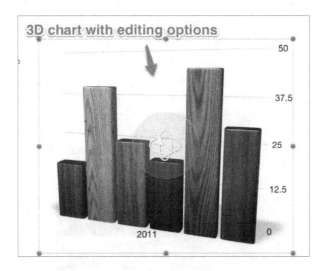

When we feel unsatisfied with our edits or when we want to try different formatting options, the **Undo** button at the top comes in handy. If you touch and hold this button, it converts to **Redo** and has an opposite function to the **Undo** button.

It would be very helpful if you tried out and practiced some object insertions or editing and formatting before moving ahead, so that you are thorough the basics of content creation.

8. It's time we should now look at animation, a very important aspect of creating presentations. To begin tap on the **Tools** button and then tap on **Transitions** and **Builds**. Now in the navigator view, tap on the slide you wish to animate. Scroll through the list of animation effects and tap on the one you wish to apply. Look at the following screenshot. The same process can be repeated for all slides. To save changes and exit from the animation view, tap on the **Done** button.

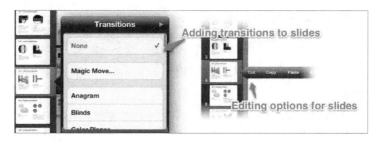

9. To play this presentation tap on the **Play** button. The presentation will open in full screen mode and all animation effects will be visible now. To navigate between slides during presentation make use of the horizontal swipe gestures. To show presentation to the class, depending on the size of the class, either use the bright screen of iPad or use the external TV adapter to connect to a display monitor.

   When you are finished presenting, pinch at any point of the slide to come out of the play mode.

10. To organize the presentations you have made, tap on the **Presentations** button in the top-left corner of the screen. The presentation manager view shows the preview of all available presentations and options to share, duplicate, and delete them. Look at the following screenshot. To open a presentation from this view tap on it. This view also lets you drag-and-drop one presentation over another to rearrange them in different folders.

11. With Keynote, it's a very easy task to share your presentations. You do not need to use other apps to upload your work and then grant access to others. You can perform all this from within the app by tapping on the **Tools** button and then tapping on **Share and Print** to e-mail, print, and export the presentation. You can also grant access to students and fellow teachers directly using iWork.com.

How it works...

Presentations and charts created through the Keynote app are saved locally on the device. These can be displayed to the class through your iPad and does not involve printing or drawing on large sheets of paper. Each student can also access these presentations after the teacher shares it. This helps while self-studying and for examination preparation.

There's more...

For any extra help and troubleshooting, use **Help** under **Tools** menu. The Keynote app opens only in landscape mode. It does not let you loose work because it automatically keeps saving changes as and when you make them!

Accessing your presentations everywhere

If you choose to use the facility, Keynote can save and sync your work across all iCloud devices, so you can pick up from where you left the last time.

For presentations imported from Mac's Keynote to iPad's Keynote, custom fonts will be converted into Helvetica on the iPad due to the limited number of fonts available on it.

Magic Move

Magic Move is a special animation effect of the Keynote app. It allows the user to animate objects between different sets of positions on two different slides. To apply Magic Move to your slide, select it from the list of animations that appear in the **Animations** view. Say yes to duplicating your slide and follow the on-screen instructions to set initial and final positions of your objects.

Other chart-making apps

Keynote provides much more than just creating charts. If all you want to do is to make charts, you can also try Quick Graph and Easy Chart apps. Both these apps are free. While Quick Graph supports more complex charting, Easy Chart is very convenient to create and share simple charts.

Carrying your textbooks (Must know)

Paperbooks are expensive to produce and to buy. This recipe will advocate the use of **iBooks** instead of paper textbooks. These books often come with multimedia features such as video and audio media, photo galleries, links, and so on. With iBooks corrections and updates are also free, eliminating the need to buy a new version every year. Most of the big publishers have their books available on iBooks or on other eBook apps. These eBook apps also support features such as notes-taking, highlighting, flash card creation, and the like, which are especially helpful for teachers.

Getting ready

If you are using the latest version of iOS in your iPad you should already have it on home screen. If not, start by downloading iBooks app from the App Store.

How to do it...

1. Open iBooks app from home screen of you iPad. Now tap on **Store** from top-left side of the screen. This will take you to iBookstore. Under **iBooks TextBooks** you can browse the available books subject-wise or look up for a particular title using **Search** textbox and view full details of a book. The next screenshot shows these facilities:

When you buy a book it will show up under **Library** as shown in the next screenshot:

2. The fantastic retina display of the iPad makes the text appear like that of a magazine. To modify the view for your convenience, you can change the brightness, text-size, font, and reading theme from within the app using editing options in the top right portion of the screen.

3. Most of us are used to highlighting or underlining text while going through a book. iBooks provides this feature in an iBook! Highlighting in iBooks is easy—just tap and scroll through the text you would like to highlight. This option also lets you add notes clipped to parts of text. You can use these notes to turn them into flashcards for class lessons.

4. Another task we often have to do while reading a book is to look up a word in the dictionary. In iBooks, if you don't know the meaning of a word, tap on it and its glossary will appear with the definition! You can even open the **Dictionary** option from here to learn more about the word. This is shown in the following screenshot:

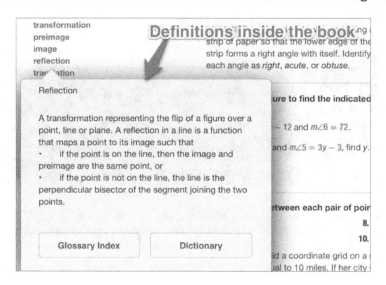

5. Readers can either view the book content in a traditional textbook format or in a graphic-enhanced format. What makes iBooks amazing and much more useful than a paper-textbook is the reader interactivity it offers. iBooks can play videos and 3D animation inside a book page as shown in the next screenshot. It can make tables and figures full screen and easy to read.

Many books also have interactive charts and figures, which can make understanding physics and biology much simpler. The following screenshot gives us an example. Likewise many geography textbooks have interactive map exercises, where the reader can use the drag-and-drop feature to perform these exercises.

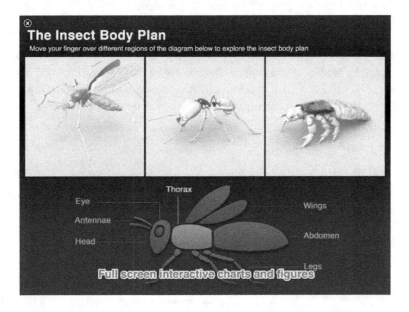

All these features hold high importance in situations where a teacher wants to demonstrate something in class, without actually having to arrange for a laboratory setup. With such features complex science topics become very easy for students to understand.

6. When you feel like someone should read out the book to you, the iPad presents itself. You can use the **Voiceover** feature to have iPad read the book's text to you.

How it works...

When the user downloads a book from the iBookstore, it is stored in the device and can be accessed anytime and anywhere, not requiring the user to be online. These iBooks are not only replacement for, but enhancement to the paper-textbooks due to all their interactive features. These books are stored, organized, and displayed in iBooks library just as a teacher would like his/her library to be.

There's more...

You can always download a sample part of a book from iBookstore before buying full copy. You can also get updates to books for no extra charge.

Top K-12 publishers are on iBooks

K-12 major publishers such as McGraw-Hill, Pearson Education, and Houghton Harcourt have already made most of their books available on iBooks for $14.99 or less.

iCloud sync

iBooks is iCloud-enabled which means it can sync all your books, notes, bookmarks, and purchases across all Apple devices, which is ideal if you use many of them.

Recording attendance and student profiles (Must know)

It seems hard to imagine a regular teacher without an attendance record book which he/she opens daily to call out names. But this task will enable teachers to change this perception through use of explicit teacher-oriented apps such as Attendance2 and Teacher's Assistant Pro to track students' attendance, behavior, infractions, and achievements quickly and easily. Incidents on students' behavior and achievement can be documented in real time and reports can be sent to parents and administrators instantly via e-mail. These apps also support complex classroom grading and management.

Getting ready

Download the latest version of Attendance2 from the App Store. It costs $4.99. Attendance2 is a universal app that runs on iPad, iPhone, and iTouch.

How to do it...

1. As we always do it, we will begin by launching the Attendance2 app on the iPad. You will now see the home screen of your app. Tap on the **Add** (**+**) button in the top-left corner of this screen. This will take you to the **Add new course** view where you can add all the courses you are teaching. You will find these courses appear under the **Courses/Groups** section on the home screen of Attendance2 app as shown in the next screenshot:

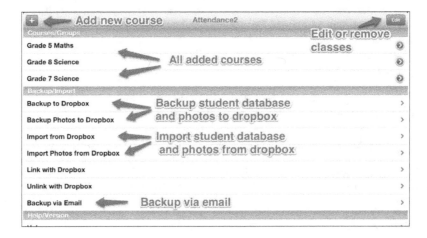

2. Let's now add information about those, maintaining records of the students. You can add students' records manually but the easiest way is to export the records as `.csv` files from your student database and save this file to your Dropbox folder. Import this `.csv` file via **Import from Dropbox** option of the app home screen. Such options are shown in the following screenshot. Attendance2 also lets you add a photo for each student, this being especially useful while learning names of students in a new class.

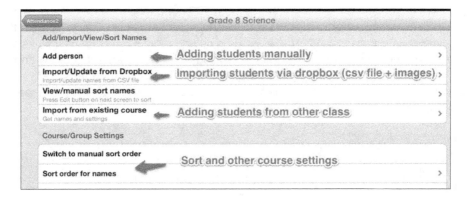

3. Let's now look at how you will be using this app on a daily basis in a classroom. Attendance2 is pretty simple to use. Tap on the class you want to mark attendance for, add a new date, and start marking students **Present** or **Absent**. In case your entire class is present on a day, you can use the **Present** button on top-right side to mark the presence of the whole class and save yourself some work of iterating through the entire student list. This is shown in the next screenshot:

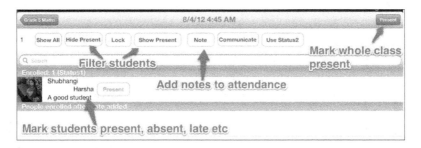

As we discussed in the task introduction, Attendance2 can do something more than just marking attendance. This app also lets you take notes for a class or for a student. The notes you create associated to students can prove helpful to point to them while taking attendance or otherwise. In the previous screenshot, the **Note** button in the top bar of the screen lets you add these notes.

4. Let's now take a look at how you can communicate your attendance records or other information to your students or their guardians. Attendance2 lets you e-mail attendance reports as `.csv` files, which can be opened in Excel or numbers. You can also send e-mails with other information to all students or to selected group of students depending on whether they are present or absent on a certain day. To e-mail, click on the **Communicate** button from your course attendance record of a particular to day. You can now view all e-mail options, select the desired one from the list, and create an e-mail.

5. You can also send individual attendance records for students via e-mail. Look at the following example. If you also use your iPhone for this purpose, it will let you SMS attendance reports from within the app.

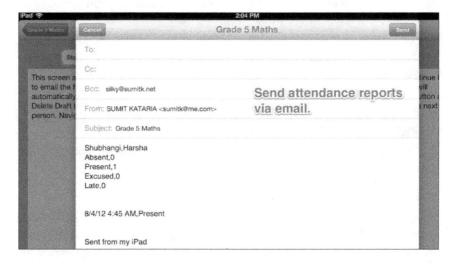

Send attendance reports via email.

6. You can even set filters on viewing students. Using **Show All**, **Hide Present** and **Show Present** buttons, you can selectively view all absentees or those present in the class respectively.

How it works...

Attendance2 stores all attendance records in a database on your device. The database file can be imported, retrieved, edited, and exported as per user's needs. The attendance records created provide easy navigation and look up options, thus helping a teacher to stay better organized.

There's more...

Attendance2 is one of the many apps available for the iPad to log attendance. It has a simple and easy to use interface and solves the issues related to attendance recording. However, there are other apps in the App Store that might let you do even more!

Teacher's Assistant Pro to log student behavior

Teacher's Assistant Pro app lets teachers log student actions, achievements, and behavior in classroom. It lets you store all parents' and students' details in the same system and also lets you e-mail them directly with student information from within the app.

Making quick references (Must know)

Every teacher must have come across this situation many times; a student pops up a question and you say you will get back the next day with more information. How would you like if at this moment, you have at your fingertips, near infinite information about almost every topic in the world. As they say, the best things in the world are free, and all the best apps that give such power to teachers are free! In this recipe let's look at the Safari app to make quick references over the entire World Wide Web. We will also have a quick look on using WordWeb and Encyclopedia Britannica apps to make topic-wise lookups.

Getting ready

The Safari app is present in your iPad on the home screen. What you need to download is WordWeb and Encyclopedia Britannica apps that are free.

How to do it...

1. Let's begin by using the Safari app to surf the Internet. Launch the app from the home screen of your device. Enter the URL you want to visit in the address bar and hit Return. Your web page will load.

2. If you are looking for a quick Google search, just enter your search term in the **Google** search box at the top-right space and hit Return. Google search results will load.

3. Using Safari is pretty simple and that is what makes it powerful if you are looking to make a genuinely quick reference! Safari offers some other basic features of a web browser. It's time we get familiarized with them.

4. While surfing the Internet moving back and forward are the most common tasks. Use the **Left** and **Right arrow** buttons respectively to navigate to the previous and next web pages.

5. The feature we are now going to see is of particular interest to teachers. It's the reading list. The **Book** icon opens up your reading list in a pop-up menu. To add a web page to the reading list, tap on the **Add** (**+**) button on the top-right corner of this pop-up menu. You can view the web pages on your reading list filtered by their read-status. Bookmarks of your browser can also be accessed from this pop-up window by tapping on the **Bookmarks** button at the top-left corner.

6. Safari supports tabs for viewing multiple web pages. The **Add Tab** (**+**) button on the right-hand side of all tabs lets you open a new tab in the app.

How it works...

The Safari app opens up the entire World Wide Web to a teacher and a host of information arranged in websites and web pages can be found and accessed here. The Google search bar at the top bar makes it even quicker to refer to a topic. A teacher thus has all information handy at all times!

There's more...

The Safari app is a web browser that lets you browse the Internet and gather information on a topic. There are however more apps that are dedicated to word and topic lookups.

WordWeb: the free offline dictionary

As we talked about earlier in the recipe, WordWeb is a free app. WordWeb is more than just a dictionary. It has all the features of a thesaurus and also speaks out words to let the users know the correct pronunciations. If you feel WordWeb is providing you with just too much information, you can customize what all information you want to view for a word in the **Settings** page.

What makes WordWeb all the more awesome is that an active Internet connection is not required to use it! All information comes with the app and is stored on your device when you download the app. Whether you are on a field trip, in the school bus, or in a classroom, you can quickly have all information about a word without having to worry about the availability of Wi-Fi hot-spots.

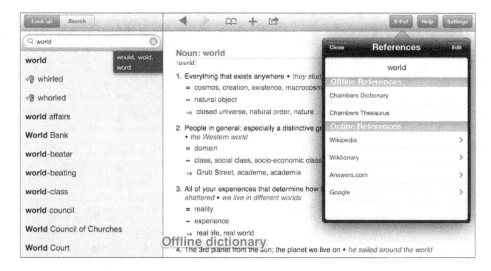

Encyclopedia Britannica

Encyclopedia Britannica is again a free app but requires the user to purchase a subscription. The subscription is available at a nominal price of $1.99 per month, which can be purchased through iTunes account and gives access to all information and features that the app has to offer.

Almost every topic on this encyclopedia is supported with high quality pictures, charts, and diagrams and the Encyclopedia Britannica is very reliable and written by field experts.

The app provides convenience features such as searching for topics, marking pages as favorites, customizing viewing options, and so on, to make the user experience all the more wonderful and easy. See the next screenshot:

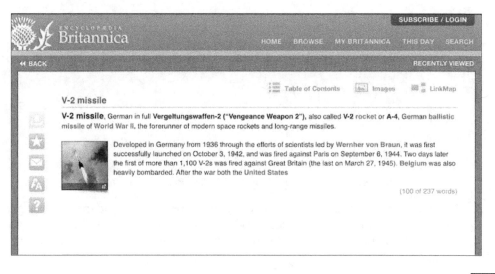

Using projectors and interacting (Must know)

Lecturing with projector and slides is one of the most common methods of teaching. There are many ways to connect your iPad to classroom's projector system to do presentations. In this recipe we will discuss how to mirror whatever is on your iPad's screen—presentations, web pages, or apps to your HDTV, VGA, or HDMI compatible projectors or other compatible displays. The recipe will enable you to share the vast and well-presented information available in various iPad apps with the class.

Getting ready

The Apple VGA adapter is a must for this recipe and it is shown in the following diagram. Other optional hardware is Apple Digital AV Connector (HDMI), HDMI to VGA Adapter, and Apple TV. You can purchase all these connectors from the Apple store or other retailers.

How to do it...

1. Apple VGA adapter or Digital AV connector can be used to display an iPad's content on projectors, monitor displays, or compatible TV. Most of the available apps are set to mirror same content as of the iPad device, unless they are designed to behave differently for external displays. For example, Videos app sends video content using video out and Photos app sends slideshow of photos to an external display. Similarly Keynote app can be used to do classroom presentations using mirroring/video-out by connecting your iPad to display devices using the afore-mentioned adapter.

2. To get more information on whether an app supports video mirroring or video out, refer to the app's details page on iTunes.

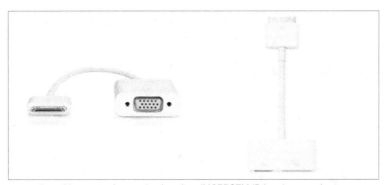

http://store.apple.com/us/product/MC552ZM/B/apple-vga-adapter

3. Attach the smaller end of the Apple VGA adapter to your iPad and the other bigger end to a VGA compatible projector or TV. Automatically your iPad's screen is mirrored to the VGA compatible display. Whatever you do on your iPad can now be seen by your entire class.

How it works...

Contents of your iPad are seen on a bigger screen through the Apple VGA adapter. This way, all students of the class can clearly see the information you wanted to share with them on your iPad. This will give you the power to play videos, interactive diagrams, and display high quality images with the tap of a finger to the entire class.

There's more...

Apart from just mirroring everything to an ordinary display device and keeping your iPad at a fixed place, there is something more you can do.

Apple TV

Apple TV can be used to connect your iPad wirelessly to projector. This will make your lecture experience completely mobile. You can share your iPad's screen via Apple TV using AirPlay mirroring. AirPlay mirroring is only available in iPad2 or above with iOS5. You will also require the second or third generation Apple TV. The last requirement is that your iPad and Apple TV should be on the same wireless network. You will attach your Apple TV to your HDMI compatible projector or convert Apple TV's HDMI output to VGA via HDMI to VGA adapter and then connect the projector using that VGA adapter. The Kanex ATV Pro, also available in the Apple store is very useful for connecting an iPad to Apple TV. These connectors are shown in the next image:

To enable air mirroring, double-tap on the **Home** button of your iPad. On scrolling towards left-hand side you will see a button to share screen, shown as follows:

You will see all available display options from where you can tap and select **Apple TV** and turn **Mirroring** to **On**. When you want to disable mirroring the same option should be used to turn it **Off**.

Troubleshooting

If you face any troubles connecting your iPad to projector, disconnect the VGA adapter and reconnect. Check if your cable is intact and not detached at any point.

A word of caution: accessories that convert VGA or HDMI signals to other video formats are not supported by iPad. Make sure you are using iPad2+ and iOS5.1 or above for this recipe.

Connecting with your subject (Must know)

Videos, pictures, and interactive diagrams can make a conventional blackboard and textbook teaching class very interesting. This recipe will help teachers know their subjects better, teach their subjects with interactive resources, and make their students learn subjects in a fun and interesting way. Here we will look at various apps of popular school subjects and see how they can help in being an effective teaching aid.

Getting ready

There is a good collection of education apps in the Wolfram Course Assistant Apps. For the purpose of learning, let us begin by downloading one app of each subject. From the App Store, download MathRef for mathematics, Chemistry Pro: Chemistry Tutor for chemistry, Wolfram Physics I Course Assistant for physics, Muscle & Bone Anatomy 3D for biology, and World Atlas HD for geography.

How to do it...

1. Let us begin by connecting with mathematics. The MathRef app includes over 1400 helpful formulas, figures, tips, and examples of equations and concepts. Launch the MathRef app and you will see a list of topics on the left-hand side. Look at the next screenshot:

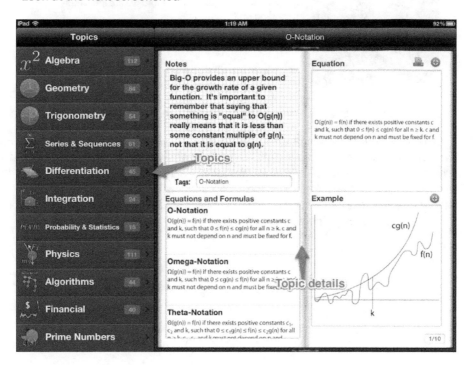

2. When you tap on a topic from the list its details open up. In the details view, you can see the topic's definition, properties, and so on along with other details. Just tap on the detail you want to view and it opens up in the right space. To go back to the list of topics, use the **Topics** button on the top-left corner and when you are done reading the topic, you can use the **Done** button in the top-right corner of the screen. The app also lets you share a topic's page with your fellow teachers or your students. To share, click on the **Share** button at the bottom of the screen. The following two screenshots show MathRef home screen with a list of topics and a detailed view of a topic.

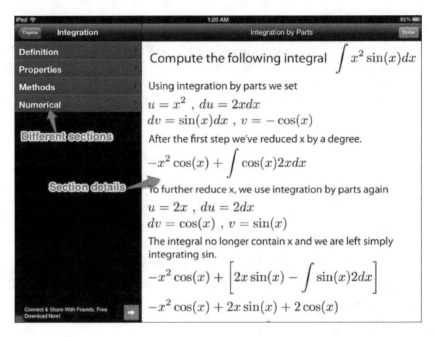

It's time now to get to know your science subjects in a different and better manner.

3. The Chemistry Pro app we downloaded has an exclusive lesson library with several videos that acts as a fantastic repository for AP and General Chemistry. As you launch the app you will see a list of lessons available. Each lesson is in the form of a video. The video starts when you tap on the corresponding lesson name from the left-hand side panel list. You can view this video in full screen for convenience. The next diagram gives you an idea how the screen will look:

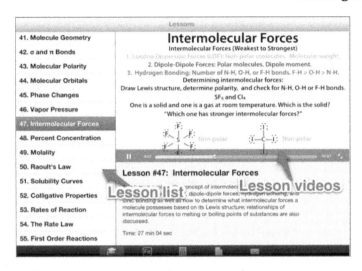

4. The Chemistry Pro app also provides chemistry flashcards, tools, and equation sheets. These can be viewed from the respective tabs at the bottom of the screen. To view the answer of a flashcard tap on it and it flips around to show the answer. Swipe the finger to the left- or right-hand side to navigate between the flashcards.

5. When you click on **Tools** tab, you will see the periodic table open up. On the top-left corner, you will see the **Molar Mass Calculator** button. Tap on this button and a calculator will open up. Just type your elements and hit *Enter* and the app will calculate the molecular mass. The **Unit Converter** that can be opened from the top-right corner of the screen provides easy unit conversion. The periodic table you see is also an interactive one. Tap on any element, and you can see its molecular mass and other basic details at the top part of the screen:

Let's now look at a physics app. The Wolfram Physics I Course Assistant app is ideal for teaching and for making quick references to introductory physics. It contains numerical problems and their detailed solutions with graphs and charts.

6. On launching Wolfram Physics I Course Assistant app you will see a list of topics on the left-hand side. Tap on any topic to learn more about it. When the detail view of a topic opens up, you will see a numerical problem or concept titles on the left-hand side panel. The details of a concept, including a definition and description, appear in the right-hand side panel of the app.

7. For a numerical problem, you can specify the value and unit of an attribute from the drop-down lists. After specifying values and units tap on the **Compute** button. The computation takes place live over the server and the solution along with relevant graphs comes up in the right-hand side panel. It is important to stay connected to the Internet to use this app. The next screenshot shows a numerical problem along with its detailed solution:

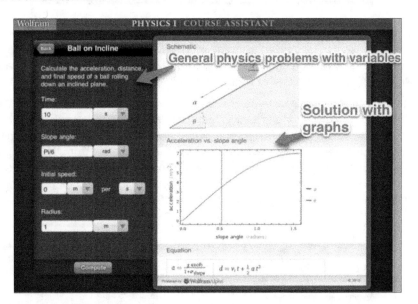

Now comes the third main component of Science—biology! There are several apps for biology, some even dedicated to specific topics. The app we have at hand here for demo, the Muscle & Bone Anatomy 3D app, is an extremely fascinating app that shows the human musculoskeletal system in 3D views and truly embodies digital education!

8. Launch the app and you will find a simple neat UI open before you with an illicit diagram of the human body. Tap on any muscle label to view its name, action, origin, insertion, nerve supply, and comments in the left-hand side panel as shown in this screenshot:

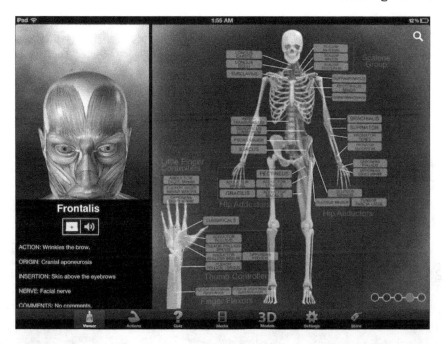

9. The **Actions** tab will show the human body divided into muscle sections. Tap on any section and choose an action from the list which appears, to see the action animation and details. Look at the next example:

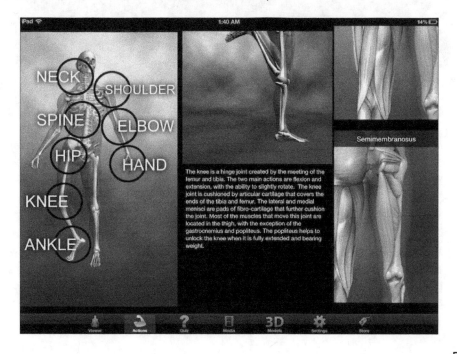

10. The **Quiz** tab will let you conduct various types of pre-made and adaptive quizzes in class, thus lessening your burden to create lengthy quizzes! The **Media** tab will let you view and show information about various bones and muscles and related videos to the class.

11. To learn or to make your class learn the human musculoskeletal structure in the most amazing way, use the **Models** tab. There are seven 3D models available that you can view in the 3D space and read all associated details alongside each part. Look at this example:

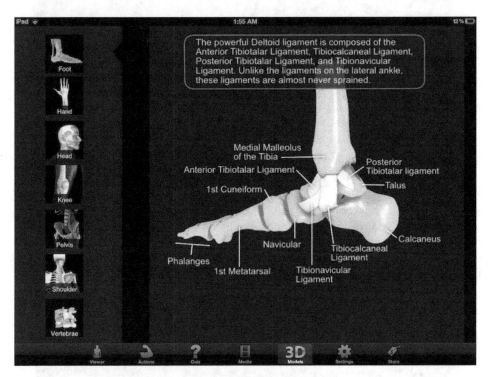

After mathematics and science, its geography that's next on our list of popular school subjects. The World Atlas HD app has beautiful and precise set of maps of the entire world sketched out in great detail. The first screen of the app is the globe of the world. The app works only when connected to the Internet. However you can search and download maps in the **Map Library** to access them anytime offline. You can bookmark a map, zoom-in, and zoom-out using respective buttons.

12. To view the map of a specific country or place, either navigate through list of **Nations & Territories** or search using the **Search** bar at the top-right corner. All maps can be viewed in several layers that can be selected from the bottom tabs. The next screenshot gives an idea about this:

13. An interesting feature that makes World Atlas HD even more useful is that it provides facts and figures of almost all places. Just touch-and-hold on a place on a map and a popup showing the country's flag, facts, geographic, and socio-economic data will appear.

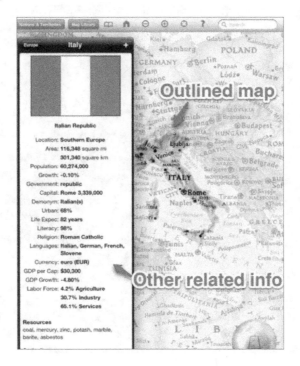

How it works...

Digital education apps provide aid to teachers and helps them and their students to better connect with subjects. The videos, interactive charts, and diagrams make the classroom interesting. It proves to be a very convenient teaching method for teachers, where they don't need to draw complex diagrams on the blackboard and have a source of subject-specific lookup and problem sets always at their fingertips.

There's more...

The apps we discussed previously are just a few out of the subject-specific apps available. There are many other apps available for teacher as well as student aid.

The Molecules app for chemistry

I want to add Molecules app here because it is one of the most amazing education resources apps available. This free app will let you view molecular structures in 3D. These structures can be one of the six default molecules present in the app, molecule structures downloaded from the RCSB Protein Data Bank, or your own custom molecules in a compatible file format. You can view all molecules in ball-and-stick and space-filling visualization modes that can be selected from the top-right corner of the screen. You can pinch by two fingers to zoom in and out on the structure and move your fingers across the display to rotate it.

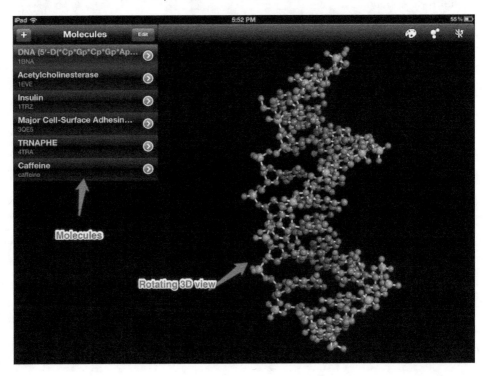

Search for your subject

There are innumerable apps in the App Store for subject-wise education. All you need to do to find your desired app is to search for your subject in the App Store, and choose from the options available that suit your needs best. It is always a good idea to begin with free apps if you are not sure about the exact content you are looking for in your subject app.

Creating and managing timetables (Must know)

Like all teachers, you will be juggling between classes, making notes on the homework of each class, noting down assignments to be given or collected, managing your papers to do all these tasks, and then wishing someone could just remind you of all this when your class is beginning. We have the iPad to fulfill this wish of yours. In this recipe we will look at the Classes, a simple app that will let you conveniently manage your weekly timetable and associated class information.

Getting ready

As always, let us get ready to use Classes by downloading it from the App Store. To begin with, it is preferable to download the Classes Lite version that provides all features of the full version but limits the number of subjects, classes, and homework. The Lite version is free while the complete version costs $0.69, which is also pretty cheap.

How to do it...

1. Launch the Classes Lite app from your iPad home screen and you will see your weekly timetable directly open up in a clear and simple landscape format. As it is your first launch of the app, you will see your timetable blank.

2. To add a class to your timetable, tap on the **Add** (**+**) button on top of the timetable. A popup appears where you can specify the class details such as the subject, location, instructor, timings, class frequency, and reminder options. Tap on the **Done** button after specifying all details to save this class and place it on your timetable. You can repeat this process for adding more classes. The number of classes that you can add are limited in the Lite version but the full version lets you add unlimited number of classes. The following screenshot of the Classes Lite app depicts this class addition process:

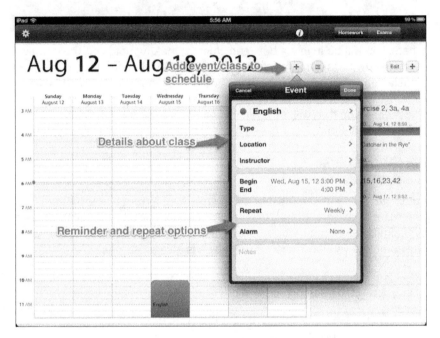

3. You must have planned some content, homework, or assignment for your classes. To add this information, use the Add Task (**+**) button on the extreme right edge of the screen. In the popup that appears, specify the task's subject, due date, content, type, and so on and tap on the **Done** button after specifying all details. The task addition popup is illustrated in the next screenshot:

4. After creating a timetable for you, let's look at the app settings and extra tasks you can specify. Tap on the Settings (gear) button at the top-left corner of the screen and a pop-up window with different settings options will open up. You can have a preview at these options in the next screenshot:

Different available app settings

5. You can specify your list of subjects, types, and instructors here. Display can be customized using the **Display** option. The **Manage Data** is one of the most useful features. Using this feature you can e-mail your timetable to yourself to create backup with the **Create Backup** option or even to your students to keep them updated with the latest changes. The timetable is e-mailed in the form of an attachment that can be opened from the Classes app on an iOS device. The entire timetable can be cleared off from here by tapping on **Delete Data**. This is shown in the next screenshot:

Backup app's data

How it works...

All your classes and related information is in one place in the Classes app and you get reminders of all of your classes. This way, you don't miss out on your lectures and make your students do in class what you have actually planned for them!

There's more...

Apart from Classes, there is another app—Timetable Pad which can let you manage your timetable in a simple, effective manner.

Timetable Pad

The Timetable Pad app costs $1.99 and is also a timetable creation app with different colors to mark different subjects. Apart from class details and notes entry, this app lets you share your timetable via e-mail or print with an AirPrint enabled printer. It provides text suggestions for quicker text entry and even a provision to create two weekly timetables for those with alternating schedules.

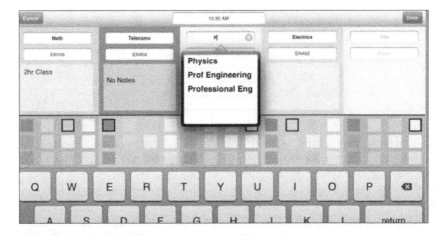

Interactive books for kids (Should know)

Children learn very fast when they are taught interactively. Interactive books make this very convenient and effective on an iPad. In this recipe, we will look at creating interactive books for kids and accessing the huge collection of such books on the iPad. Interactive books are ideal for auditory learners and for struggling readers. It is the best way to club learning and entertainment and creates a fictitious world for the child during story reading, thus teaching a child much more than just reading language.

Getting ready

We will be looking at the Demibooks® Composer app here to create and read interactive books. Let's open the App Store and download this app, which is available for free as part of an introductory offer by Demibooks Inc.

How to do it...

1. Let's create a simple interactive book on iPad. On the first screen of the app, tap on the **New Book** button to start creating your interactive book.

2. On the book creation screen, you will find a quick navigation bar at the bottom. Just click on the preview of a page or section to navigate to it. It will look something similar to the next screenshot:

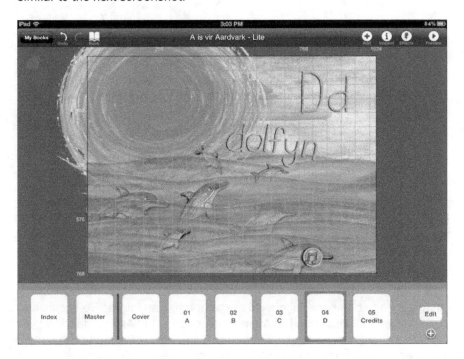

3. We now need to specify the general details of the book such as its name, icon, category, and the like. To do this, tap on the **Book** menu and specify details in the popup which comes up below the menu button as shown in the next screenshot:

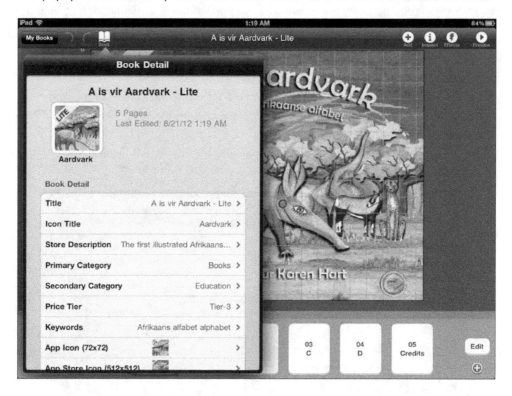

4. Good content is what makes a book a success. Let's now move on the major part of book creation—content creation! To add text, tap on the **Add** button and choose **Text**. A text area will open up where you can place your text and conveniently format it. Similarly images and movie clips can be added using the **Add** button.

5. Animation and other special effects are what make an interactive book stand apart from conventional eBooks. The **Animation** option in the **Add** menu will let you import individual image frames and animate them. A number of animation options are provided in this app to let you create very close to what you imagined. This option is shown in the next screenshot:

6. To make our book really interactive, we need to make it react to user actions. To make a book element reactive, tap on that element to select it and then use the **Behavior Editor** located in the **Effects** menu. In **Behavior Editor**, specify the name of the behavior, the user action to respond to (in the **If** field) and the action to be performed in response to user action (in the **Then** field). The user and the book reaction are both chosen from a decent list of actions that the app provides.

7. You can preview your book content along with all effects using the **Preview** button.

8. Also you can view and read your collection of interactive books using the **My Books** library.

How it works...

By specifying animation and other effects to each element of the book, we make our book interactive. Even when we use other interactive books available in the market, we make learning a lot of fun for small children who learn language and reading as well as effortlessly gain elementary practical knowledge of the world.

There's more...

Creating interactive books involves a lot of effort. Pre-made interactive books are great when you need to make kids learn classic children's stories and other basic information.

Interactive touch books for kids

This free app is a collection of 50 interactive books for children aged from 18 months to 10 years. The app comes with three free books in its collection, while the other interactive books can be bought from within the app at reasonable prices. Apart from books, this app also comes with a free video collection for children.

Stand-alone interactive books

There are plenty of interactive books available in the App Store. These books do not need a separate viewer app and behave like stand-alone apps. Most of children's classics are now available as interactive books. *Alice for the iPad*, *Old Macdonald Had A Farm*, *PopOut! The Tale of Peter Rabbit*, and *Toy Story Read-Along* are few popular ones amongst the large number of interactive books available for the iPad. The following picture is from the interactive book Old Macdonald Had A Farm:

Educating students with special needs (Should know)

The iPad is not just a fancy device people can use for their entertainment or to make their usual daily tasks slightly more convenient. This device can make a significant difference in the lives of disabled children who are in the process of learning. Disabled students can develop and enhance their communication and social skills, and even learn to adapt to real-world situations and respond to them promptly. In this recipe we will cover iPad apps that will help teachers to make this difference in the lives of their disabled students.

Getting ready

Let us download the LetterReflex and LanguageBuilder apps from the App Store. They cost $2.99 and $3.99 respectively.

How to do it...

1. The LetterReflex app is a helpful tool for children with Dyslexia who face letter reversal problems as the biggest hurdle in the start of their learning process.

2. On launching, this award-winning app provides you with two activity options: **Tilt it** and **Flip it**. Tap on **Tilt it** to start this activity. The activity requires the user to tilt the device to get the on-screen ball into the marked holes associated with reversible letters. This kinesthetic form of learning helps associate left- and right-hand sides with letter recognition. The activity will take you through a series of levels of this game and the score is logged in the device as you complete the levels. At the end of each level, its score and accuracy is displayed and you can choose to repeat the level, or go to the next level depending on the score you initially targeted at. You can always use the **Back** button at the bottom–right corner of the screen to go back to the home screen. The next screenshot shows how this activity looks on screen:

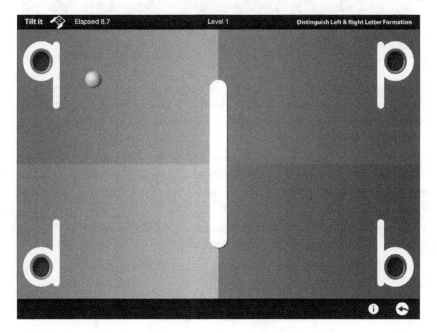

3. To start the **Flip it** activity, tap on **Flip it** from the home screen. The levels and scoring arrangement is same as that for the Tilt it activity. This activity challenges kids to match the correct orientation of words and letters by visually discriminating and manipulating them. Look at the next example:

4. To report a student's progress to his/her parents/guardians or to keep a record of all students for yourself, you should use the **Report** button on the home screen. The **Report** screen will show the activity log along with options to e-mail the log or to clear it completely for a fresh beginning.

5. Let us now look at another award winning app—the LanguageBuilder which helps special needs children with autism spectrum disorders or sensory processing disorders. Ample use of audio recordings and clips can help improve the auditory processing of these children.

6. The **Settings** tab of this app will let you specify student's name, select a suitable theme, and choose an apt hint level depending on the student's skills.

7. The main activity lies in the **Play** tab. This activity will present a set of images belonging to a particular theme along with incomplete sentences related to the image. The student should complete these sentences. The **Record** button will enable you to start/stop recording the student's answer. The **Hint** button will provide hints according to your chosen level in settings. You can repeatedly play the child's recorded sentence to let him/her take in and analyze the response. The **Save Recording** button will save the answer. You can then move on to the **Next Image button** and continue the same process to get to the end of the activity. The next screenshot illustrates these options:

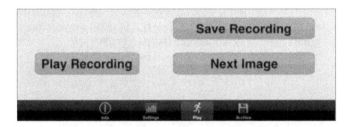

8. All the saved recordings the child can be accessed from the **Archive** tab. You can choose a sentence from the list in the left-hand side panel and then play it using **Play the Saved Sentence**, delete it with **Delete**, or you can even share it using **Share** with the child's parents/guardians or tutors. By playing saved sentences from the archives repeatedly, the child understands his own auditory responses better and tends to show improvement over time. The teacher should assist the students during the repeated hearing process to guide him/her about what the response is to and whether it is correct or not, or if it needs improvements.

How it works...

The LetterReflex app helps dyslexic children understand the difference between left- and right-hand sides and associate letters with correct direction to overcome the letter reversal problem. The LanguageBuilder app stresses on building the auditory response and analysis of a specially enabled child by recording and repeatedly playing the child's own audio clips.

The interactive activity structure of both these apps makes learning easier for the child by clubbing fun with education. The real-world images and themes of the LanguageBuilder app help the child learn something extra about practical life stuff also.

There's more...

There are iPad apps dedicated to assist the specially enabled people in their daily tasks.

Proloquo2Go and SpeechTree

Proloquo2go is a fantastic communication assistant for children with speaking difficulties. It provides smart text-to-speech conversion features with very natural voices. Users can choose from a huge vocabulary available in the app. This vocabulary is arranged into groups of words, and while building sentences, words are highlighted intelligently by the app. User can also write custom sentences if required and all these sentences are effortlessly converted to speech by this app. The app costs a hefty $189.99 but is extremely helpful for some specially enabled people. The next screenshot shows a preview of this app:

Image source: iPad App Store

SpeechTree is another expensive ($169.99) yet amazing communication assistant and helps people with complex communication disorders.

Teaching art, craft, and practical skills (Should know)

Learning and experimenting with art becomes all the more fun when you can undo your actions, zoom and rotate your art, and even share your creative piece instantly with the world. iPad wins over art on paper when all these factors are taken into account. And if you ever want to convert your artwork to the paper form, just print it out! Let's now look at a couple of iPad apps that can make teaching artwork easy and more effective.

Getting ready

Download Animation Desk™, Procreate – Sketch, paint, create and SketchBook Pro apps from the App Store. The first two apps cost $4.99 each while SketchBook Pro costs just $1.99.

How to do it...

To begin with, let's look at the SketchBook Pro app which has a simple yet powerful user interface. It has a decent range of sketching and painting tools and suits amateurs and professional artists alike. All tools and menus reside in the top bar of the app screen, giving the user a big and neat working canvas. This is shown in the following screenshot. The app provides multiple canvas sizes, the facility to work with multiple layers and a huge variety of brushes and color tools.

The right-most button in the toolbar gives you the facility to work with **Layers**. The third-right **Text** button is to insert text into your artwork. This text can be formatted with the help of text toolbar which comes up at the bottom of the screen when **Text** option is selected. The **Brushes** button in the middle of the toolbar presents a variety of brushes and their colors. A preview of these can be seen in the next screenshot:

1. The **Undo** and **Redo** buttons are simple but most useful when you want to undo the mistakes you commit or when you just want to try out different painting options.

2. The SketchBook app makes file handling easy. You can save your artwork and view it by using the **Gallery** button. Once inside the gallery, you can organize and share all your files.

3. Another popular sketching and painting app is Procreate. Procreate has a dedicated painting engine which makes the painting experience fast and professional. Tools of this app are present in the top and right sidebars and are pretty similar to the ones we just discussed in the Sketchbook app. The smudge feature of this app which can be accessed from the **Smudge** button, located right next to the **Brushes** button makes your drawing get a canvas painting type effect with blending colors. Here are a series of screenshots to give you a preview of the basic tools provided in the app:

Those were apps for static painting and sketching. Let's take our learning level one step further by looking at animation creation app, the Animation Desk™ app. The concept and creation of animation is easy to teach and learn using this app. The artist creates a series of **Frames** (paintings) here to turn it into an animation. This is exactly what professional animators do. To create a painting (a single frame), this app provides lot of tools present on both the sides and bottom of the work-area.

The app also provides a set of dynamic and static backgrounds and other pre-made objects to get students started quickly. Animation being almost every child's fascination, teaching its basics in art classes is a good method to keep attention of students.

4. As you create frames, they start appearing on the preview scroll at the bottom of the screen. To select and work on any frame, simply tap on it to make it active in the work area. To add sound to your animation, use the **Sound Track** button at the bottom-left corner of the screen.

How it works...

Teaching artwork on an iPad gives both teachers and students more power and flexibility to work and modify specific parts of the painting, commit mistakes, and learn from them. The range of painting and sketching tools provided in a single app to create every piece of artwork is much more than that can be available to students at the same time in an art class.

There's more...

We looked at apps for teaching art and craft, but to make them work effectively in a classroom we need to make use of a couple of teaching aids.

Aids for art teaching

As you demonstrate creating a piece of an art, you will need to use a large display screen. Your iPad screen can be mirrored to a larger one using Airplay which we learnt to use in a previous recipe. Be it sharing your demo art with the students or getting your students to submit their weekly artwork, a file-sharing app is a must! Dropbox, the popular file-sharing app is the ideal solution for both these tasks.

Teaching music on iPad (Advanced)

iPad lets you play all the instruments you want at the touch of your fingers. If you are a music teacher, you don't need to depend on sets of musical instruments for your students learn music because all of them are there in your sleek device! You can record a piece of music, play it repeatedly, modify this saved piece, and let your students also experiment with it and record their own creations. What we are going to look at in this recipe is an app, which is a complete recording studio in itself with a decent range of touch musical instruments to create your music piece.

Getting ready

Download the $4.99 GarageBand app from the App Store, which is the main app we will be looking at.

How to do it...

1. The first thing you see when you open GarageBand is the Instrument Browser. You can swipe the screen to browse through the various available touch instruments and tap on any one of them to open it. Let's take up the **Grand Piano** as our first demo instrument. Look at the following screenshot.

2. In **Grand Piano**, you see the piano keys in the bottom-half of the screen. The GarageBand acknowledges dynamics just like a real piano does. It differentiates your soft touch from a hard tap and plays sound according to the pressure with which you touch the keys.

3. A real piano is incomplete without the pedal. The pedal prevents the sound from echoing. In the GarageBand piano, the **Sustain** button does this! Just tap and hold the **Sustain** button to lock it. Try to create some music now and you will find the echo gone!

4. Tap on the **Grand Piano** button in the middle of screen to see a number of built-in sounds. Tap on any option to implement it. You will see a complete change of looks of your screen and the screen will have all controls such as draw-bars that your selected instrument has.

5. What your screen shows are a limited number of nodes. Use the arrow buttons to access all octaves of your piano and you will notice a change in the sound of the keys as per the active octave. This way you can access all nodes of your keyboard.

6. To go back to the Instrument Browser, use the **Instruments** button. Let's look at another musical instrument now—the drums! How hard you touch a drum or a bell corresponds to how hard you would have been hitting on them if you had a drum-stick in your hand. Look at the following arrangement of drums:

If your students are very young and have problems managing a physical drum-set, the GarageBand might be just the solution you are looking for!

7. The top bar of the screen remains the same for any instrument you pick to play. The small red **Record** button on this bar lets you record the music you create. As you record, you will see a timeline appear just below this top button bar. Use the Play button to listen to your last recorded piece of music.

8. If your students don't have any previous experience with music and you are just looking at giving them a playful idea of playing instruments, you can make use of the series of GarageBand Smart musical instruments. For instance, you can pick the Smart Guitar from Instrument Browser. In the Smart Guitar, you will see pre-built combinations of nodes over the chords. Your students can play these nodes individually or in series. An even easier playing option is using Autoplay. Point the Autoplay selector to a value from 1 to 5 to activate this mode. Now tapping on any combination will automatically play all nodes in it.

9. Your recorded pieces of music can be combined and organized to create a song. An interesting way to keep your students engaged and motivated will be to allocate them different musical instruments to create some music and then combine those pieces to form your class song. You can combine up to eight tracks of same or different musical instruments to form a song. The **My Songs** button of the top bar will take you to a song management screen where you will see your recorded pieces of music along with their respective instruments and timelines. You can use your finger touch to move and crop the music pieces from their timeline. Swipe from left- to right-hand side over any instrument row to open the **Mixing Board** for all tracks of the song. All your changes are auto-saved.

How it works...

The GarageBand app lets you and your students create music on all instruments without actually having to arrange for expensive and huge musical instruments. The music mixing and modifying options given by this app provide you with a complete recording studio inside your sleek device and accessible on your fingertips.

There's more...

Let's look at two more apps for composing music.

Creating music for dance

The KORG iElectribe app simulates the historic KORG Electribe-R which was used for many years for composing music for dance. This app creates music just as it was on the KORG Electribe's sound engine and also provides options to choose from a number of sound effects.

Recreating the KORG MS-20

Another app which recreates another of the KORG musical instruments is the KORG iMS-20 app. As its name suggests, it simulates the KORG MS-20. This app features a MS-20 monophonic synthesizer, a drum machine, an analog sequencer, a mixer, and a song composer.

Teaching using 3D resources (Advanced)

3D demonstrations and videos make any classroom lively and interesting. Adding 3D to your conventional teaching method can make your lessons more captivating and engaging. You can use 3D supporting iPad apps in your class to help your students understand complex topics such as the human body or the solar system very easily. In this recipe we will look at the Solar Walk – 3D Solar System model app in detail, which uses 3D demonstrations along with vast amounts of factual information to explain the complex solar system.

Getting ready

Download the Solar Walk – 3D Solar System app (costing $0.99) from the iPad App Store. Also arrange for a pair of cyan-red 3D glasses each for your students and yourself.

How to do it...

1. As you launch this app, serene music welcomes you to the journey into space. The following screenshot shows the space. You can navigate from the Sun to the end of the galaxy by zooming in and back by zooming out, both using pinch by two fingers. During your zooming in to reach from one point to another in the galaxy, you will pass through all planets and even their moons that will come in your way just as if you were actually traveling between those two places.

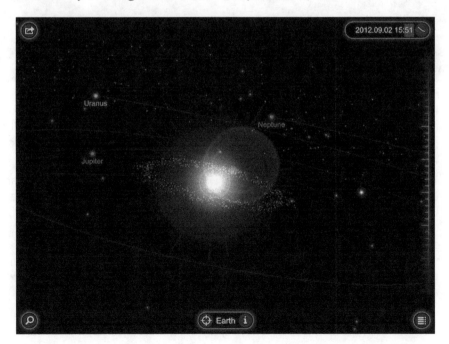

2. You can use your fingers to rotate the solar system model on all three axes. To view a planet in details, just tap on that planet. You will see a detailed model of that planet open up before you along with its full information. The **General Information** tab contains information such as the planet's name, size, mass, and so on. The **Internal Structure** tab will illustrate the planet's composition layers. A slideshow of the planet's actual pictures will be there at the bottom of this screen showing planet in detail.

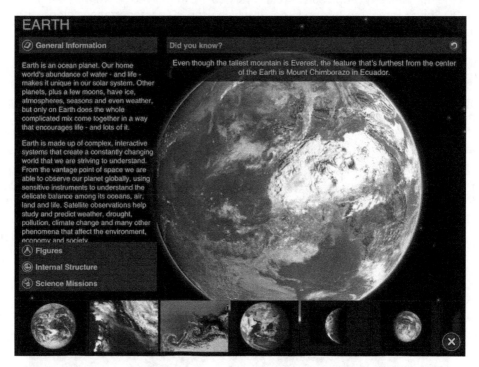

3. In this app, you can see the planets move in real time. If this is too slow for you, you can move fast in time. You can also go back and forth in time to see the position of all planetary bodies at that point of time. The time you are at in the app is visible at all times on the top right corner of the screen.

4. There is a decent library of educational videos present within the app. You can access this library and a couple of more app features from the **Options** button located in the bottom-right corner of the screen. All videos in this library are also available in 3D. But to view these videos in 3D, it is required to make use of the 3D glasses we arranged for before beginning this section. These videos are also interactive along with being 3D. This app lets you bring the Sci-fi movie type space traveling experience right into your classroom. Just imagine, how much your students will look forward to attending to your class from now on!

5. If you want to send the app's info to your students for reference, or want to share your awesome teaching method with your fellow teachers, just use the **Share** button present at the top-left corner of the screen. Apart from e-mailing information and sharing it online, you can save images to your iPad's camera roll or print information to distribute notes to your students. The various sharing options can be seen in the next screenshot:

6. You can connect your iPad to your Apple TV 2 even wirelessly to make the whole experience of solar walk available to your entire class on a large screen.

How it works...

3D videos and demonstrations will not only make your class interesting, but also enable your students to learn about the planets, their moons, their science missions, and other details of the solar system. The 3D experience will make you and your students feel like you all actually walking in space, going to planets, and the Sun and getting know them personally.

There's more...

The human body is one of the most complex systems that exists in the world. Understanding this system can be made simpler using 3D modeling.

Visible Body 3D Human Anatomy Atlas

A boon for biology teachers and students, the Visible Body 3D Human Anatomy Atlas app will let you view the human body skeletal, muscular, and neural structures (both male and female) in a 3D model. As with the solar system model in the Solar Walk app, in the Visible Body app you can rotate the human body model in all three axes and tap to view detailed information of body parts. The next screenshot obtained from the iPad App Store shows a preview of the Visible Body app.

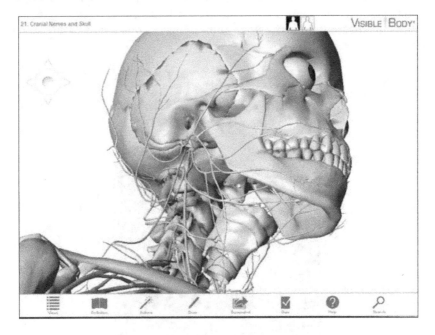

Publishing your learning material (Advanced)

We are now at the advanced level of teaching with an iPad and it's a perfect time for you to learn to create your own custom content and share it with your class. This content creation in the form of creating your own book will put you in the driving seat and give you great command over your class. Till now, we discussed downloading and reading books on the iPad, but in this recipe you will learn to create, share, and publish your own books that can be read on your iPad.

Getting ready

Download iBooks Author on your Mac. It is the most popular Mac app for creation of interactive eBooks and is available in the App Store. To create simple books on the iPad itself, download the Book Creator app from the iPad App Store. Book Creator costs $4.99 while the iBooks Author app is free.

How to do it...

1. To create your own interactive books and make them accessible to your entire class on your iPad, we will learn to use the iBooks Author app. On its launch, the app will show you few pre-made book templates. You can pick a template for an easy head start to creating to your first iPad book. The main screen of the app will look something like in the next screenshot:

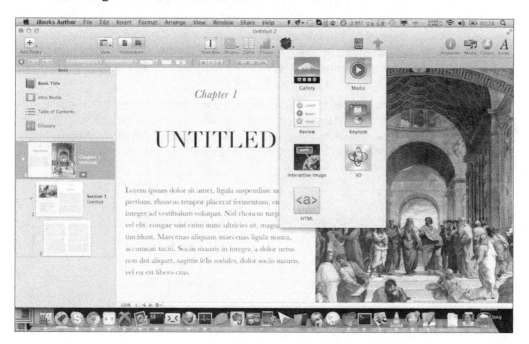

2. The left-hand side panel shows the preview of the book pages in correct order and chapter organization. You can tap on the appropriate heading to specify the title of your book, its multimedia introduction, table of contents, and your book's glossary.

3. To add a new page to your book, tap on the **Add Pages** button. The page you choose to add can be a new chapter, a new section to an existing chapter, or just another page to an existing section in a book chapter. The drop-down menu which appears on tapping the **Add Pages** button can be previewed in the next screenshot:

4. As you start creating content for your book, you will need to add text, images, charts, and tables to the pages of your book. You can add these elements from the top bar of the app.

5. Let's make your first book interactive and interesting. To add interactive elements to a page of your book, tap on the **Widgets** button. A drop-down menu will appear and you can pick the desired element here. The two fundamental media elements—images and videos can be added by using the **Gallery** and **Media** options respectively. As the name suggests, the **Interactive Image** icon will take you to a widget to create your own interactive images and add them to your book.

6. You can preview your book at any point on your iPad. To preview, connect your iPad to your Mac through the USB cable and make sure that iBooks is open on your iPad. Now tap on the **Preview** button and you will see iBooks open on your iPad with your newly created book as part of your collection of books as shown in the next screenshot:

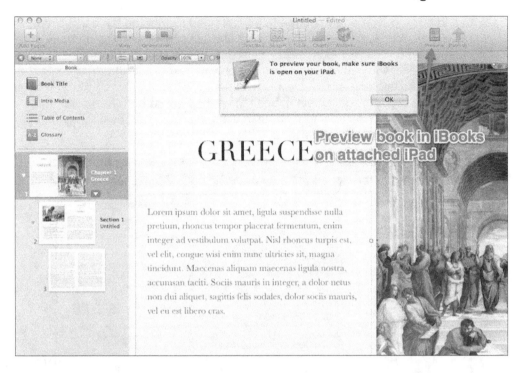

7. To publish your book on the iBookstore, use the **Publish** button and follow the steps that appear on your Mac screen. Once your book is approved and published, your students and other people can download and view your book on their respective iPads.

8. iBooks Author requires a Mac to create books. But if you are looking to create quick, relatively simple books, use the Book Creator app which lets you do everything on your iPad itself. The first screen which appears on your iPad as you launch the Book Creator app is the collection of your books. Tap on the **New Book** button to start creating your book.

9. The first thing you should create is your cover page! The set of buttons of the left-hand side of the top bar will let you add images and text to your pages and format them. To begin with, let's put an image on the cover page. Tap on the **Image** button and choose an image from the drop–down list which appears. You can use image handles to resize or reposition this image.

10. To add text tap on the third button from right-hand side of the top bar. A simple basic text editor will come where you should type your text and tap on **Done** once you have typed your complete text. This text is placed on your cover page. Just as with an image, you can resize and reposition your text block with text handles. You might be thinking—placing text is not enough, what about the text formatting!! To format a block of text, select it, and tap on the **Format** button (second from right-hand side). A range of formatting options will come up. You can see these options in the following screenshot:

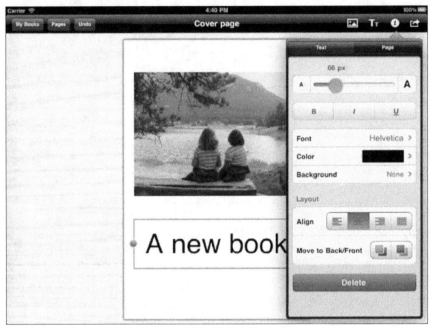

Image Source: Official Book Creator Demo

11. To proceed to creating the main content of your book—the pages, tap on **Next** near your screen's right-hand side edge. Now you can create pages of your book and add text and images to them in the same way we added to the cover page. To navigate between pages, use the arrows present near the edges on the left- and right-hand sides of the screen.

12. As the name suggests, the **Undo** button will let you undo any action or mistake you made while creating content on any page of the book.

13. If at any point, you want to go back to your collection of books or preview the book you are currently working on in iBooks, tap on the **My Books** button and your collection of books, which appeared as the first screen of the app, will come up.

14. To view your book in iBooks, select the book by tapping on it and tap on the **Open In** button (second from left-hand side at the bottom of the screen). Now click on **iBooks** and iBooks will open up showing your book as part of your iBooks bookshelf.

How it works...

The iBooks Author app will enable you to create powerful interactive books. These books can be viewed on your iPad, shown to your entire class and used as a great teaching aid, totally customized to suit your course needs. The Book Creator will also let you do the same but without the interactive images part. So if you are just looking to create some simple text and image books, Book Creator will be an ideal choice!

There's more...

Let's go through some basics of publishing the books you just created on iBooks Author.

Publishing your book

After completing your book on iBooks Author, you can export your book as a PDF, text file, or `.ibooks` file. If you want to sell your book which is in `.ibooks` format, you should use the iBookstore to sell it. If you want your book to be available for free, you can distribute your work anywhere you like and in any format.

To publish your book at the iBookstore, you need to sign up for iTunes Connect. If you are interested in selling this book, you will also need to complete a separate application form for this purpose, which is available on Apple's support website.

Details on how to create and publish updates to your existing books on iBookstore can also be found on the Apple support website.

Learning iPad tips and tricks (Advanced)

Through our journey of this book, we looked at various apps that will surely make your teaching easier, interesting, and very resourceful. In this recipe we will look at a special app which will give us a few basic tips and tricks for working on the iPad. These tricks are aimed at making your regular work on the iPad easier.

Getting ready

Download the Tips and Tricks - iPad Secrets app from the iPad App Store. This useful app costs just $0.99.

How to do it...

The app we are looking at here is a very simple app to use. In fact, making your iPad easier, smoother and more enjoyable is what this app aims to do.

1. When you launch the app, you see a book of tips and tricks in front of you. Reading and scrolling through this book is simple. You can flip through its pages just as you would do in iBooks. Every page of this book has a nice unique trick explained for you.

2. Every trick is very well illustrated with a high quality screenshot or picture and an easy to understand explanation. Wherever applicable, the top-right corner of the page will show the iOS version on which the tip will work. For example, the Print Center tip shown in the following image works only for iOS version 4.2 or above and the same is indicated in the top-right corner of the screen.

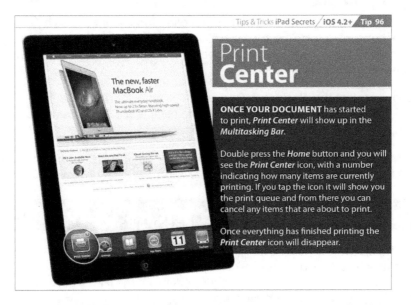

3. Let us now quickly look at bottom controls of this app. You can see this button bar in the following screenshot. From left-hand side, the buttons are **Chapters**, **Favorite**, **Settings**, **Gift App**, **Tweet this Tip** and **Email this Tip**.

4. The tips in this app are arranged in the form of chapters, pertaining to the function they perform. The **Chapters** button lets you pick up a chapter of your interest or as per your requirement. Look at the next screenshot:

5. The **Favorites** button or the star button is to mark/unmark a tip to your favorites list. You can view this list as the first chapter in table of contents which opens from the **Chapters** button.

6. The next button which is the **Settings** button lets you control the sound which plays on flipping the book pages. You can also contact the developer or rate the app through this button.

7. Now as you go through this app, at many instances, you might recognize trick you were talking about the other day with your friend or colleague. You will want to quickly tell your friend that you have found a solution and explain it. You can do this easily by using the **Email this Tip** or **Tweet this Tip** buttons.

8. If you like this app and are feeling generous, you might just want to gift this app to a friend of yours. Use the **Gift App** to satisfy this generosity of yours!

How it works...

The Tips and Tricks - iPad Secrets app will teach you many useful tricks for using your iPad. These will make your regular jobs on the iPad much more efficient and easy.

iTunes U (Advanced)

In the last recipe of this book we will look at iTunes U, an app by Apple which will not only give you access to courseware of most of the top notch universities and colleges worldwide, but also will let you manage the courseware for yourself in a very convenient way. Books and all media resources for a particular course are clubbed at one place in the iTunes U app. Apart from accessing existing courseware, you can create your own courseware and share it with your students.

Getting ready

Download the free iTunes U app from the iPad App Store.

How to do it...

1. On its launch, the iTunes U app will look just like the iBooks app with a bookshelf containing courses you have subscribed to.

2. You can edit your course collection using **Edit** to remove some courses or use the **Catalog** button to subscribe to more courses and add them to your course collection. When you tap on **Catalog**, the screen flips to show you the catalog of available courses. The following screenshot is from this catalog. You can tap on any course to see its complete description, outline, and ratings from students who have already subscribed to that course. Tap on the **Subscribe** button to subscribe to this course.

3. Let's now look at how to use a course that you have already subscribed to. From your collection of courses, tap on a course to open it. You will see four tabs on the right-hand side of your course book. The first tab of **Info** shows you all the information about the course. This information is organized under various topics such as course outline, course instructor, and the like, listed in the left-hand side panel. The left-hand side panel will always show you the list of topics under any selected tab.

4. The **Posts** tab lists all the posts or messages of the teacher to all the students in the class. These posts also include class assignments. Whenever a new post is added to the course, a notification appears. Tap on a post to read it. If for example, an assignment asks you to read a particular book, then you can directly access that book from this post. Just tap on the icon of the book and iBooks will open it for you. Just as on a paper-book, while reading you can highlight any text or material you find important! When you are done with reading the book, you can switch back to the iTunes U app and tick-mark the assignment as completed. If an assignment asks you to watch a video, just tap on that video link, the video will automatically start streaming and you can watch it then and there. The next image shows the posts tab of the **CS50: Intro to Computer Science** course.

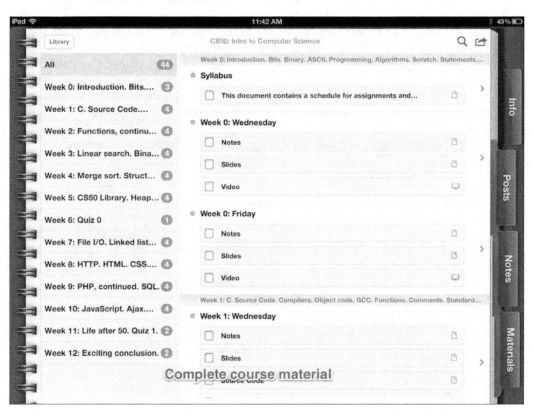

5. The **Notes** tab gathers your notes and highlighted stuff from all your courses and books at one place. You can tap on a note to view it or even to add further text to it.

6. The **Materials** tab shows all the available material of that particular course. This material can include audio clips, video clips, books, documents, and even other iPad apps. In the case of a course lecture, you can download it for offline viewing at your convenience using the **Download** button. Videos, audios, books, and apps can be directly accessed and downloaded from within the app. Look at the next screenshot:

7. To go back to your collection of courses at any point in the app, use the **Library** buttons present at the top-left corner of your courseware.

How it works...

iTunes U gives you access to organized course resources from around the globe. When you use these resources, you teach better and may even learn something more than you already knew!

There's more...

You can create your own courseware and upload it to be accessible at iTunes U for your students and others.

Creating your own course

To create your own courseware, you should have your own valid Apple ID, which you can easily create on Apple's website if you don't already have one. Open the iTunes U Course Manager Portal at `https://itunesu.itunes.apple.com/coursemanager/` and log in with your Apple ID. You can now create your own course on this portal. If you want to share your course at any time with a limited number of people, use the **Share Course** button to copy your course's link and then e-mail this link to your targeted audience. When you want your course to appear in the iTunes U Catalog, use the **Submit Course** to iTunes U Catalog button on the **Course Settings** page to send your course for publishing.

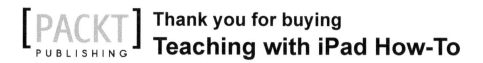

Thank you for buying
Teaching with iPad How-To

About Packt Publishing

Packt, pronounced 'packed', published its first book "*Mastering phpMyAdmin for Effective MySQL Management*" in April 2004 and subsequently continued to specialize in publishing highly focused books on specific technologies and solutions.

Our books and publications share the experiences of your fellow IT professionals in adapting and customizing today's systems, applications, and frameworks. Our solution based books give you the knowledge and power to customize the software and technologies you're using to get the job done. Packt books are more specific and less general than the IT books you have seen in the past. Our unique business model allows us to bring you more focused information, giving you more of what you need to know, and less of what you don't.

Packt is a modern, yet unique publishing company, which focuses on producing quality, cutting-edge books for communities of developers, administrators, and newbies alike. For more information, please visit our website: www.packtpub.com.

Writing for Packt

We welcome all inquiries from people who are interested in authoring. Book proposals should be sent to author@packtpub.com. If your book idea is still at an early stage and you would like to discuss it first before writing a formal book proposal, contact us; one of our commissioning editors will get in touch with you.

We're not just looking for published authors; if you have strong technical skills but no writing experience, our experienced editors can help you develop a writing career, or simply get some additional reward for your expertise.

Moodle 2 for Teaching 7-14 Year Olds Beginner's Guide

ISBN: 978-1-84951-832-1   Paperback: 258 pages

Effective e-learning for younger students, using Moodle as your classroom assistant

1. Ideal for teachers new to Moodle: easy to follow and abundantly illustrated with screenshots of the solutions you'll build

2. Go paperless! Put your lessons online and grade them anywhere, anytime

3. Engage and motivate your students with games, quizzes, movies, blogs and podcasts the whole class can participate in

Articulate Studio Cookbook

ISBN: 978-1-84969-308-0   Paperback: 245 pages

Create professional training courses with Articulate studio's strong interactivity and rich content capabilities; all within the familiarity of micro PowerPoint

1. Complete your courses by creating Flash-ready presentations through familiar PowerPoint

2. Employ Articulate Engage, Quizmaker and Encoder to make dazzling interaction, asses learners and add full-motion videos

3. Practical recipes to get you moving on a specific activity without the extra fluff

Please check **www.PacktPub.com** for information on our titles

www.ingramcontent.com/pod-product-compliance
Lightning Source LLC
LaVergne TN
LVHW080103070326
832902LV00014B/2396